Anne Haverty's previous collection, *The Beauty Of The Moon*, was a Poetry Book Society Recommendation. Her novels include *The Far Side Of A Kiss* and *The Free and Easy*. Her classic biography, *Constance Markievicz: Irish Revolutionary*, has been re-published in a new edition. A member of Aosdána, she lives in Dublin.

A Break in the Journey

A Break in the Journey

Poems

Anne Haverty

NEW ISLAND

A BREAK IN THE JOURNEY
First published in 2018 by
New Island Books
16 Priory Hall Office Park
Stillorgan
County Dublin
Republic of Ireland

www.newisland.ie

Print ISBN: 978-1-84840-672-8
Epub ISBN: 978-1-84840-673-5
Mobi ISBN: 978-1-84840-674-2

Typeset by JVR Creative India
Cover design by Mariel Deegan
Printed by

New Island received financial assistance from The Arts Council (An Chomhairle Ealaíon), 70 Merrion Square, Dublin 2, Ireland.

New Island Books is a member of Publishing Ireland.

Contents

For

Anthony Cronin,

beloved,

as ever

The Nun and the Greyhound

A nun and a greyhound
would come to the door, one
to the hall, one to the back,
lean, ardent, lonely and sad.

Both in retirement, the nun
and the hound. She
from the classroom, he
from the track.

One found it hard to talk.
The other never barked.

Though once they were boss.
In convent and kennel,
bursar and winner,
flying down the corridor, or up
the field, alarming the children,
lithe, forbidding and cross.

That we brought out
the good porcelain
meant nothing to the nun.
The dog ignored the bone.
All they wanted now the position
of household pet – this
mute longing impossibly
greater than tea
or a timid embrace.

They came to the door
too late,
the greyhound and the nun.
Too late
to be consoled,
to be taken in.

Poor Ladeen

Each plays their part.

The farmer fetches
the mattress and the rug
he keeps especially in a shed
for poor beasts facing the cut,
makes a bed for the ewe
on the smoothest flag.

The vet is cheerful and quick,
as clever with the needle as with the knife.

And the black-faced ewe
though her belly is slit
stops quiet as they ask
and lets

them search out her he-lamb, blood-streaked,
and coax him to his feet.

They rub him down with straw
and an old coat,
and watch him go, eagerly
tottering into the world,
his first glimpse
of the pale western sun.

Another new-born
hurrying along
behind his quick-to-recover
sheep mother
to his little sojourn
in an upland field
hung between sea-cliff
and mountainy rock

between new grass
and the butcher's block.

Poor ladeen, the farmer murmurs,

fervent and harsh, like a man
whose hard-earned wisdom is still fresh.

Poor ladeen.

At the Pier

Viewed remotely
from his mountain fields
the infinite sea
below in the bay
is shades of moonstone
mild and far away.

Today a visitant
to town
he drops his
black Raleigh bike
against the sea wall,
to watch up close
the water's swell.

Shy Wicklow chap. A
martyr to the blush
in his summer mac
and his Sunday cap

down from the hill
for 'the messages',
his weekly necessities.
And today as well
town business.
The doctor or the dentist ...
Possibly the solicitor
about that case.

Raptly watching
the breakers
gorge on the beached stones,
docile and pale
he flushes
at the voracity
of their desire.

Under their spell
surging
in him again

the urge
to be gone.
The old bike
ditched. The bag
hugging the carrier
with the cornflakes
the Baby Power
and the John Player Blues.
The doctor's admonition
and the solicitor's grin.

The old itch.
To take off.
Anywhere.
Anywhere at all
only it be far.

Far from home,
from pedalling the empty
mountain roads,
from the hillside graves.
From the milk
souring in the jug.

6

India

1

Hearing
the languid song
of birds
you look up
and see

like the slices of lime
deftly placed
on the gold rim
of your glass
by that extravagant
barista in the big hotel

three
green parakeets
resting
on a sun gilded wire

2

Like enormous cloths
afloat in the gloom
winter mists
meet warm vapours
from the dahl-pans
kids are stirring
with tireless vigour
on the smoking fires
of the outdoor kitchens,

stirring
with the vigour of the poor
who know
that today

today they got lucky.

And from wherever –
who knows from where –
a railway siding,
the dried up culvert
under the Sofitel,
that daily beat on the corner of a street
where the tuc tucs
pause when the lights are red –
khaki'ed crowds are gathering

like a dishevelled,
starving
and losing army.

In hempen wraps,
patched up
from sacks too holed
for porting chilies and rice,
wraiths in earth-
stained shrouds,

faces released
from the extravagant
smiles
they paid out all day
to put together
rupees enough to buy
this night's supper.

To accept
your state
their betters say
is a tenet of their faith.
They're accepting,
grateful even
for the life
they got.

But
In Delhi's parks
under the bitter dark
of sudden night
standing
to grimly eat
melancholy and apart

they are not
accepting this.

Marriage

Like a small ship
The bathroom is lit.

She is undressing.

She is taking off
her face

to go to bed

as away on the billows of the sea

with him.

Strange

Finding myself
in Aarhus
I pay a call
on our Viking cousin

Grauballe Man.
So ancient a chap
so venerable with age
he is granted a title.

Not that he cares.
Nestled in the roomy
leatherette pyjamas
of his bog-soaked skin
he rests in his long long sleep.

I gaze at him
(he couldn't give a toss)
and find there's nobody
I know
no kith or kin
of mine
I can trace
in his turf-tanned face.

And yet I find
him no stranger
no more strange
than our own
often not at all anonymous
dead.

But the stave-church!
The stave-church in Aarhus
is strange,
so strange and other.

Shrouded in mist
among alien trees,
those blunt-hewn timbers
blackened
by the eldritch fires
of Nordic ice.

That horned roof.

And daubed ochre and red
a circus of serpents
gaudily swooping
under the eaves ...

But it's only a pastiche!
A reconstruction
of a Viking church
half-way in time
between the bog-man's
and mine –
yet more bizarre
than Araby
or old Cathay.

No, it's not our selves
that make us strange.

It's what we make
and what we do
that make us strangers
me or you

and from each other
look away.

Grief

Pale sunlight
falling on a white cup.

Even in grief
we can sup.

Why does it have a look
of hope
this reflected glow?

Even in grief
we can love.

Oh, Our Fragile Lives

In the morning the heating went
And with it our lovely
Pre-revolutionary world.

Inside an hour or two
They had gone, our metaphorical girls,
Who metaphorically
Fill the metaphorical coal-scuttles
And the metaphorical hot-water pails and
Keep the fires metaphorically
Going, upstairs and down,
Had left us on our own.
And shivering in a mass of ill-matched
Woollens we huddle by the struggling grate.

Bravely trundling turf
Home in a trolley, we're like refugees,
Our life reduced
To the pathos of what could fit
In a couple of sacks.

Down the chimney the wind
Whines, jealous
As a siege of wolves.
And down the telephone we
Howl. We're living in an ice-box.
It's Siberia here.
An alien air is rising through the cracks.

Still, behind it all, behind
The misery of the not-warm,
We know, we're strangely confident
That the gas repairman must soon come.

And with him our lovely girls, warming
The rooms as they've always done.

Poemless

What a poem
you could have made
that night –
preparing to retire
in a grim impasse
somewhere around Châtelet les Halles.

Between the restaurants'
kitchen entries, dingy and neon-lit,
and the noisome waste-bins reeking of fish,
you had made your bed, laid
out white sheets on the ground.

Foraging in the blanket
you found your hairbrush and swept
your hair.
Not quite the hundred strokes
the beauty-books advised
but half at least.
And then your nightgown, demurely
pink. Qualmly
modest you shimmled in, and
sighed and composed
yourself for sleep,
resigned as a guest
in a bad hotel – after
giving us two, when you looked
over and found us watching,
the two fingers.

Sales voyeurs! Chiants!

We felt the shame –
though we might protest as well
that the rules of etiquette
are not clear as yet
regarding our unhoused.
And you presenting
for all we knew
a public
display of performance art.

But look, it never would
come off, that poem of you.

It lacked a room,

a basin,

a real bed.

The Dog Will Not Take Gloom

The dog will not take gloom,
he refuses to look on a melancholy face.

If I indulge in despondency or tears,
he who lies constantly at my feet
and leads the way from room to room,
takes himself off
to the neutral area of the stairs.

In fairness it works both ways. He
hides his own woes, nurses in secret
a paw or a tooth.
It may be a principle of his
that suffering is done in solitude.

Subscribing apparently to that pop belief
in positive thought, doggedly
he may know best.
Confined to cheerfulness I
find it somehow in that or this.

Innocence

You come home
From the park
Your black coat covered
In pink blossoms
From the flowering trees.

And, dear dog,
You don't know it.

Stricken While Out Walking With Man and Dog

He
Is not young
And dogs
(they say)
Do not
Have souls.

So
Perfect happiness
Is not
To be

Unless I get
Positive
Proof

That we three

Will walk again
In the fields
Of Elyse

Beautiful Day at Birkenau

Even then,
Surely even then,
There must have been
Days at Birkenau
As beautiful
As this.

And even then,
On such a day,
It was surely inevitable
That you
Could sense again,
Just for a moment,
The clemency
Of things.

Beyond the watch-tower
And the black-fanged fence,
Clemency.
In the sunlit grass, in the sun
Hazy over a wood,
Its leaves
Painted that October red
You remember
From the Matisse print
Eva brought home
That time
From Paris.
Some clemency even
In the church spire that rises
Beyond the wood.

And when the vixen
Paused to scratch her ear
And met your eye
For a moment
Before loping away
Across the basking plain
After a hen or a hare,
You saw
The freedom
And the rightness
Of an animal's stride.

But then the daily
Anguish
Grips you again.

Here
Is no clemency.
No clemency
In humankind.

In the Etheric Spaces of the Web a Microchip

Translates from the Portuguese the story of a Novel

Between the entrenchment
And the curse – it was
This that I made.
Of an agricultural scene the contours
Of the tragedy –
The protagonist wanders as a phantom
And, wild in one motor,
Runs for the fields and
The empty nights.

Its history advances
In a duel between different forces
Of Abel and Cain, under
The appearance of the diplomacy.
In culminating of the madness
That of it takes possession, underneath
Of its tree of contemplation

And mirage.
The rustic voices and environs
Populate the narration of one,
Murmur that it is colour and dither
– The round and cinereous forms
Of the sheep to graze,
The naked and blueish branches

Above my head
With the fingers
To be lost in the mist. Spots
Of moss in the rind
Against which bracket the head. Moss
Of winter, yellow-severed. As Chartreuse,

One of these drinks of party, that I
Ordered to the waiter
Underneath seated
Of the awnings of canvas
To the stretches blue and white
Of Deauville –

And my white hands already of the winter.

Porn

At dusk
in a window
a boy
in a room
home from school.

The room is blue.

His mum picked the paint.

Duck Egg, Celestial.
'I want a colour
with a nostalgic feel'.

The boy
could be you

decades ago.

Immersed in words
lost in a book

constructing
illusions. Comrades
of the desert
night-skies
the glamour
of jets.
A future
of girls
in shorts.

His face
is rapt above
a touchscreen's light.
He can touch
the world. Everything
is in there.

Today's war
Ancient methods
of harvesting corn

Porn.

A new night's dark

His shadowed heart.

Liberty Square

On the screen
yet another story
of war somewhere.
'After the battle for
Kobane, Liberty Square
is today a ruin.'

Liberty Square?

Liberty Square Thurles –
Liberty Square Thurles County Tipperary.
In the sweet vacuousness
of boring afternoons in class, writing
out in my ancient copy-book
its place and status in the world –
Munster Ireland Europe Earth
The Milky Way.

A ruin, rusty with gore –
Our Liberty Square?

Deleted. Hayes' Hotel.
Stakelums.
The L n N.

Shock, that feels
like shame. A shattered face
mirroring mine
in a shard of glass.

And the proud patriot. One
of those lofty Victorian men
perched on his column.
Devoy or Kickham,
Mitchell or Parnell.

His separated head a mess
of mud. Or is that blood?

Errant
under the street
the stiffened limbs
of beasts, brindled
and brown. They were going
to be good sellers
at the Mart.

Semolino's and Supermac's

smoking sarcophagi
in the damp January air.

Schoolgirls buried
lunch in their mouths.
The shrouds of their school
uniforms, claret and blue.

Don't, don't, the parents cry.

Ryan's, O'Connor's ...

Like a film sent into reverse,
the jewellers' trays of diamonds,
returned to the earth.

To adorn, lie though they must
at dreadful angles,
at least two Martinas.
Three Joannes. Our only
Eileen. Maureen. Bid.

Like Monica Duff, caught
dressing her window.
All bundled now
in garments of dust.

Forgetting

'Since the war'
    he said
about a distant place
    'Since the war
they're all depressed.'

And with a grim philosophy
    I shrugged. Well,
whether guilty or bereft
    you can't bring back the dead.
What can they do?
    Nothing, only
go on. Forget.

But thinking of the fields
    around Ypres – those old
killing-fields of the killer years
    smoothed over
with pretty villas and roads,
    the kids yanked
from a killing-game on screen
    to be driven, complaining
to piano class
    and the ghosts
smothered under the grass –

Was it as useless
    my horror then?
At how easy it looks
    to go on, to forget.

Far

Byron went far
far out into the lagoon.

In the winter of eighteen and twenty one
rising early he would row all alone
a lone gondolier
to the little island of San Lazzaro,
the island of the Armenian monks,
hoping to learn the Armenian tongue –
'something craggy to break upon' –
hoping

for a break in the fog.

He fails.
But who can't fail
in two damp moons to know
such an alphabet as he calls 'a Waterloo'?

And the alphabet teachers
fail him too.
The teacher-Fathers censor his work –
they tell him about the Persian and the Turk
wreaking desolation
in that place where we were all begun –
but are angry
when he puts their words
in his preface, are fearful
of retaliation from satrap or pasha.

No more he goes a-rowing.

Goes back to the night
spots around St Mark's,
the marks of his last Waterloo
prefaced in his desolate looks.

In far Armenia,
he wrote, Paradise was.
There the dove came down as the flood abated,
came to the Armenian isle
marooned like an ark
in a high church-purple fold of the Caucasus.

I too went far,
farther than Byron.
For in the autumn of two thousand and one
flying to Paradise was easily done

and roving the streets
I saw like paintings unfolding
the faces of minor saints on Armenian people.

Paradise

I hadn't read Lord Byron's letters,
I had no hopes of Paradise.

For travelling in that season
was ill-advised.
The timid or wise
slowly folded their tickets
and stayed home with their families.

Hoping only to be lucky
I fly, among members of their diaspora,
Ralph Lauren golf sweaters
nonchalantly draped over their shoulders,
over the dark

pool of the Black Sea. Over Van,
Erzurum, over the bones
of their slain ancestors, under
the wreck of a moon.

Like sparking fires, stars
over the Caucasus.
I am hoping only
that my luck will hold.
I hold no hopes of Paradise.

But, sudden and marvellous, below
the port wing is the diamante glitter
of a pastoral village,
a child's view of the Holy Land drawn
on a card at Christmas,
wrapped in the serge cloth
of night in the Orient.

Yerevan, someone murmurs.
Our ark is coming in.
And I step onto Asia, ground
ochre and packed as in a souk
where the merchants sell enigmatic powders
and sniff the land

and get,
though I've never met the animal at close quarters,
the paradisial smells
of rosewater and camels.

The Knowledge, in Armenia

To each his own bread –
Share lavash and you can be sure you and your friend
Will have a falling out.

One year in three
You take black soap and wash the household rugs –
(Like many things called black this soap is brown).

More than once around the Square
A wedding-car must not careen,
Blowing its shrill ecstatic horn.

With the wedding-pair,
You have sent only new things, certainly
Nothing the girl has used at home.
(She may take however from the china
Stored in every house under a bed, bought against the day
When china is not to be had,
The white plates from Russia with red-painted flowers.)
And after the feast – like weddings everywhere –
The 'red apple' must stain the white sheet, to show
She was chaste before.

And by the way, eat up or watch out –
The mess you leave on your plate
Reflects the face of your future bride.

On the other hand, if, when you are burning incense
The plate cracks, that is a good sign. It says
All bad spirits have left the place.

About scents – the sweetest
You may concoct at home, a mix of cheap
Perfume, French, and one from a Baltic state.
The smell of a dried walnut-leaf keeps the moth away.

Give spass to a child for stomach-ache –

You must eat every four hours in the day –

You must not swim in Sevan Lake

Whose blue reflects the eyes of God, evading
Hell, which is located between Earth and Heaven.

From a church you must withdraw
As from a king or queen
Whose countenance you always keep in view.
When asked to light some candles
For another
Never keep the change.

Nor should you lounge beneath the walnut tree
– it gives out gas. But under a mulberry
You may lie for the purpose of writing poetry.
You have yet to learn the secrets
Of the acacia, the cypress, and the bay.

Hayren

(to Nahapet Kouchak)

You write how in Old Armenia
your last night's girl
would breathe attar of a thousand roses,
her kisses spilling
like wine from the south.
And you tell how, bodice buttons undone,
her breasts shone pale as a first-bitten apple,
causing the jealous moon peeping
over the mulberry trees
to waver and dim.

No talk from you
of rank vinegar or weeds.

Well, let me say now
the fitful return of that man to me
was like a fix of heroin in a paper screw
that buys back from misery
only the grey and average day.

Though I do confess
this other's love
is like champagne, frothing
a delightful every day
to a fizz of happiness.

Souvenir

The white shirt
I wore in Yerevan,
that night I sliced a pomegranate
– a fruit crowned
like a king in a medieval tale –
and, a gillygoose,
let drop, in spite of warnings
that it would never wash out,
a bead of carmine juice –
indelible, Armenians say,
as the mark of sin on souls –
I'm wearing now.

The faint pink stain
on a sleeve, a vivid
aide-memoire of that night
in David Muradyan's
when the room seemed bathed in roses,
eating pomegranates
and sweet confit of walnuts
from little spoons,
tasting arcane theologies,
Leanid singing
songs from Belarus

and David sang that ghostly air
that must still haunt the place
like glorious, guiltless sins.

Tameda

(*a traditional Armenian toast*)

Armenijan! My dear
Armenia!

You gave me
a new land
for a muse.
Your weighty gourds and saffron grass,
pink stone, tanned earth, black rock.
Your ancient roads of earth and dust.

That whiff of the east
on the breeze.
Asia
in your pleated hills, high
impassive hills folded like skeins of silk,
and *caritas*
in your heart.

Your pastoral
dishes made on milk,
dark wombs
of churches where monks
gave birth to eerie light.
Rose-pink *kashkars* piled
against the wall, reminders
of the never-ending wheel
of ascendancy and fall,
contending for position
with Soviet artefacts.

Your leaky gas pipes, factories.
Armenijan! *Armenijan*!
What will you be
in these new times?

I wish you …
I wish for you, people
fierce and wise
like Hrant Matevossian!
Absurd and playful
as Parajanov!

I wish for you good
government. Health.

And only a few
special fields
for playing golf.

Objecting to Everything Today

Objecting
to everything today.

Crumbs
in the bed,
on the counter-top,
to eating as a necessary occupation.
Hairs in the bath, twined in the brush,
dog-hairs on the couch. And his shoes
where he tossed them,
askew under it.
The importunate dog,
the cold
drear outside
and having to take him out.
And the water too hot! Objecting
to the daily
attritional messiness
of living. And to myself
more than anything.

Yesterday's
newsprints on the chair, books
I'm in the middle of I don't want to finish.
No, don't say it!
Don't say I have a cold coming on!

Objecting to the newsreader
as he briskly reads out a rape, another
murder. To that brash
light in the sky.
And the same light failing.

I am not the raped one.
He is not the murdered.

And still today I'm objecting
to living.

The luxury of us with few troubles.

The Beds of Europe

What is Europe to do? She must keep her beds
European. And what is the European bed? Let us
first clarify what it is not. It does not, like a hotelier's bed,
pretend to be new. Nor does it try to assure you
that no other body has lain before you in that bed. And
if someone unfortunately has, this person certainly
has not overslept nor left any dent or mark.
It is not unyielding. No, the true European bed
is expansive and giving. It is the bed of a large extended
family in which generations have slept,
and got up from independent and spirited.

I give you a bit of old news straight from the mouths
of some eminent writers – they say Europe is washed up,
this time she is finished for sure, exhausted.
They've been saying it for years, for Pound already
she was the 'old bitch gone in the teeth'.
But a hard and prudent bed will not see her rise refreshed.
Europe must be firm and keep her soft beds.

Christmas Chains

Those Christmas paper-chains of yore –

Tacked along the wainscot, swooping
Above the table to meet at the light
In the centre of the ceiling,
In the parlour twined
Across the mirror over the fire –

Like some antecedent of a display
To illustrate our double-helixed DNA.

Each house had its own
Colours, like a banner – twinned
Reds and greens, purples and gold –
Spending the summers above
In the attic or on a box-room shelf,
When county hurling colours got the honours.

Inexorably the years
Passing, children upping,
Leaving. And imperceptibly the chains
Fading, like water-paints,
To indecipherable hues. Pink, lavender,
Umber, whey-mixed blues.

Drooping in their tracks, limping –
Like Stasia behind her counter in the bar
Who, up to the Christmas of ninety-nine,
With arthritic fingers was pouring still
The shaky festive jar.

Til one final January, dispersed
In flames, those
Chromosomal paper-chains.

I Mourn the Funerals

I mourn the days
 of the rare and important funerals.

Mourn the drives
 fooling with the other kids in the back, to the event.
 Its object remote, we could be trivial, light. I could
 be sure she had never, unlike us, quite lived.

Death was a zero.
 Some kind of a yellow-belly, locked out,
 keeping himself to hidden fields and distant places.
 He was afraid of our father, of the car, our house.
 The whole town was safe.

And how I could look
 unbelieving on his deed – as if he could steal a person
 and leave her face intact. Well, if he did that her family
 was superhuman – to be able to see him close in and still stand.

These days
 he owns the town. Has a skeleton key for all the cars, steals
 people who were definitely alive. He has unlatched our gate.
 A soldier whose ghastly acts are salaried by the state.

And I don't live in wartime. This is life.

Train

(Literature Express 2000 – writers travel across Europe)

Leaving behind
the windy oven of the Extramadura,

blinds flapping in a breeze
like national flags bleached into unity,

our train traverses Europe west to east
through wild foxglove, cobbled lanes and birch –

we travelling companions, international
writer-passengers, hardly better acquainted
than faces you'd only politely greet
at home in the street –

past apple-orchards, fields of cabbages and hens.

Instructed in German
to be on it at seven, compliant
and white-faced on a station platform.
Your allotted one
piece of luggage trundled away,
the morning chill, no tea
put out at the breakfast buffet

and moving on, incipiently forlorn
across the Continent's crowded
estate of violent deaths and early graves
through wafts of drying hay.

Walls burnt pinks, pewter-yellows.

Outside a town called Slupsk, in a faded
kerchief, a girl working a water-pump.

In a Lithuanian glade
a white goat tethered to a stump.

And the weird
'I lived here once' sense of deja vu.

The border towns
where the train slows, halts. And the doors are shut
and you are not let out

and your papers
are inspected by a hard-eyed *controle* who clearly
will not be won by engaging him
in talk. Zoran, the Macedonian
led away – he left his passport behind
at the desk in the second last hotel –

At times like this –
and please, our German friends, don't
take it up the wrong way –
one could be prey to the frantic
notion that it was all a mistake,
our train a reprise
of the sealed transports of the last century.
and we embarked
on a journey that must come to a fearful finish.

From the rain a hamlet looms
like an abandoned shtetl.

But thundering on, a warm
breeze again and the blinds blowing. A station
painted, as from here to Greece,
in white and lemon.

A guard atop his watch-tower arm-waves in welcome
and in a distant carriage the Macedonians are singing

and pulling in
to Mamonovo there are only ladies dancing,
costumes, bouquets, the whole fanfare. All

of Mamonovo out
to greet us with offerings of 'bread and salt'.

And together

we break sugared *challah*
in a rite of consolation.

Napoleonic

'A Vendre'
'Se Vende'

After Brussels my words gave out.
And not recognising what was for sale
I took to annexation, took
any place that seized my fancy.

Like an invader on the loose, ruthless,
I took properties big and small,
anywhere setting up house.
Lay my head down on some hapless
Pole's dralon-covered couch.

And I was that one,
a stick of bread under her arm
and clutching a sack of summer fruit
you saw climbing stone steps
slow in the heat into the dark
mouth of a communal porch.

A dog – a Portuguese dog
is friendlier you know
than the dogs of France – dozed
under the orange sun
umbrella on my balcony
high up in a dizzily modernist building
of ancient Lisbon.
I would take him for walks
out on the Sintra road, thinking
of Byron.

Facing the ocean at Bordeaux
I sat in a low grey salon, windblown,
some chateau's poorer but charming
relation. I wrote a good deal there
fortified with wine
and the delicacies of the region.

Paris I left alone.
I had taken that town before.

But took note
of how faithless we are
to rooms, and they to us, how
one image, one afternoon
is enough to fix a place.
A memory of the light
falling on a rug
all that remains
of a long and complex season.

And the dacha –
that too I did not take. The *dacha*
in Tula. The blue
fragility of boards
in a mist of birch-trees,
the hue of a beach-hut
on the Baltic,
of smoke from a *samovar*.
A proud and upstart blue
in the face of calamity, the blue of
a future I must forget.

Anecdote

'What are these trees,
their flowers for leaves?'

Leaves 'achingly lovely'
as they used to say of girls
in those novels between the wars –
the 'great wars', as they say,
of the last century.

Flowers a gorgeous concentrate
of a Portuguese twilight's
blue and pink,
showy as swizzle-sticks
hung on the pastel rim of the ocean,
a yellow Suze at six.

We are wending our way home
along the Alfama.
'You say home. And we go
only to the ho-tel' accuses Virgie.
Virgie is from Bulgaria.
Mike smiles. And I as well,
recognising the truth
that we islanders – or Irelanders –
can be at home
nowhere and never.

And so always and anywhere
winding our way.
Demanding
'what is that tree?
Its flowers for leaves ...'
'No, not lilac. Not even lilac
glows like this.'
Til, like a sea-breeze,
a rumour ruffles the line.
'Jacaranda.'
'It's a jacaranda tree.'

We nod, at once
accept that it is so,
recalling those jacarandas
that soared in many a novel
between the wars.

And carrying on down
we devour fish and ham
in the brash light
of a Lisbon tavern.
Refuge of anecdotes,
neither questions
nor answers.

At the Smolny

The empire's noble girls
were boarding at the Smolny,

Anastasias, Natashas, Olgas,
sleeping in chaste – in fact already Leninist – beds.

Learning, as Catherine
the great empress instructed

The deportment and manners
of an English duchess,

To keep a good Russian table
(really a la Francaise)

And a well-stocked mind
like their German cousins.

Were learning to rein in their spirits as they
would a horse, side-saddle,

To stop the slow slide
at home on the estate,

To bring up sons not
to drink so much vodka

And themselves to not be lazy or sad
or Chekhovianly volatile.

To balance weighty books on their heads

To sleep tight and straight in their little beds.

Until Comrade Vladimir Ilych
came to the Institute

And found the headmistress's quarters
the ideal place from which
to direct his revolution,

Liked her frugal wash-basin,
her simple bentwood chair
and big black telephone.

His lithe young soldiers strode, smoking,
the long light corridors

And at night lay by the dormitory cots
of noble girl insomniacs,

Not lying anymore like serfs lie
behind the closed doors of their masters.

'Now ...' Here the learned guide's
words turn vague and euphemistic

Inviting us to think of the headstrong boys
and those only half-tamed noble girls

Billeted together at the Smolny,
all classes suspended.

'Many found' she murmurs, 'that they knew
each other before. Often as children
they had played on the home estate.'

She didn't mean us to imagine
that disgrace or even terror ensued.

No, you sensed only excitement there
in Lenin's spare boudoir,

The tingle in the air
of history being made.

Only perhaps the trembling
of Nadia's uncle or brother

Come to fetch her, and she hunkered
with cowherd Lev or Yakov

As, through a haze of smoke
from a rudely hand-rolled cigarette,

She announces without a note
of tenderness or regret,

'Return to Tsmirinova?
Go home with you?
I'm staying here. No,
I am never going back.'

Memorial

Another town,
another welcoming party.

And here they put us
on a bus
and we are driven
to the war memorial.
They're dead keen,
insist that we
pay homage to
their fallen men.

Wanting to please –
forgetting
what we know,
or deciding
not to know it anymore –
that you can kill
and be killed
and you can destroy
and rebuild –
and still you can
do it all over again –
we play our part.

Obedient
as a schoolyard flock,
in the glaring
pallor of the Baltic summer
one after the other
we mount the steps.

I followed after
Jessica, so fair and good.
And laid, genuinely
tender and solemn,
my orchestrated
rose, blood-red,
at the foot of the tomb,
suitably grave.

And it was only later
that we saw
we had fallen

into the hands of the fallen.

Knew emotions
can be managed.
And, like lives,
be evanescent.

Those Times

1

In those times a daily stroller
on the Nevsky Prospekt,
I would drop in at the Metropole.
Standing at a marble-topped table
would take coffee and a fudge-cake
flavoured with cardamom,
admiring through the gorgeous windows
the imperial edifices, one beauty
following the last. Or tea perhaps
with that Greek whose gloomy countenance
resembled the face on an ancient Roman coin.

Later I'd stroll as far as the Literary Cafe
where Tolstoy and Dostoyevsky used to dine,
for caviar and some sweet Georgian wine.

2

Oh yes, in those times
I was a tireless drinker of cocktails
standing around in rooms
I vaguely recall
as much the same proud or wistful pastiche
of the Baroque or neo-Gothic.

Or in some President's palace
or garden, we writers feeding
like fowl when their grain is flung,
our soulful thoughts
on eel and wild-duck pates.

Wild boar. Was that
by the Vistula, at Trakei Castle?

While Tomas made once more his speech
to a Minister of the People,
describing our amazing itinerary –
if we had found the Minister
luckily at home
and not in Japan.

I ate
berries from the dacha
in Tatyana's kitchen.

3

But in those other times
there were people
who longed only
to be let remain at home.
To ghosts struggling
under the greensward,
our train must look
like a grand tour
by pampered victors
of the fields of war.

Fields of grief
all smoothed over
like a goose-down quilt
on a lumpy bed.

Our nature insists
we mustn't forget.

But if we remember –
how can we forgive?

Vodu

How vital is vodka in those cold expanses of the east. On steppe and city street alike, it assumes, for people who cannot always lay their hands on such, the form of any necessity of life, food, heat, comfort and forgetfulness. I could tell you stories. Of days when at one hour the little glass presented itself to me as my dinner, at another was my goose-down quilt. And again, oh most forlorn of times, feigned to restore to me my love.

from *Corn*
by A. Havertova (1932)

Vodu 1

Sweet little well
of melancholy, of bright
and tragic hopes, of a tale
in a state of collapse on the Prospekt,
oh, reckless little tumbler.

My jailed, my tamed Fontanka,
my own little sun
exhumed from the clouds,
carried home to glitter
hopeless and dying
in a half of a cup –

Well, if we can't eat
we can drink.

And thanks be,
like little father's arms about us
and little mother's rosy smiles,
thanks be we have vodu
to liven up
a scrag-end or the midday sausage,
to wash down
the tainted cherry.

Vodu 2

Tatyana
drinks vodka
and Masha too.
Natasha
drinks vodka
night and noon.
What good, she asks,
is salz-water
when you are cold?
Igor also
and his brothers.

For they
being far from Moscow
must have vodka
to ease that hurt.

And Katyiusha too.
For though she
lives in Moscow,
she is far from home.

Vodu 3

Over there
I found you could live
on vodu,

I was nearly
as Russian as the Russians.

In Minsk indeed
my room
alarmed me,
that way it had
of turning purple
in the night.

But my capacity
was only novitiate.
And therefore moderate.

Vodu 4

Back on the track
And trundling west
In our confused and restless and impatient places,
Sweet water
Our drink now of gratitude and choice,
I showed Dubravka
My festering mosquito bites.

'What do you expect? You must
Put on them some vodka.'
She of course is from Croatia.

Summoned from his musings
With his flask
Gallant Stefan applied the drops.
He could have been a prince with a magic potion
On a silver salver.
(The prince is for Neshe
Who likes a fairyland or heroic analogy).
By Warsaw the bites were better.

Oh yes
For any affliction,
Hunger, cold, or little Kolya's pain,
For any external or internal reaction
Take vodu.

Wintering

Does Soloveva sip
Her evening tea, her red head
Bright as the birch's
Tinsel saffron
In this season?
Katya surveying
With her enigmatic smile
The grim walls
of Kalinin's Garden?

The ragged arcs of trees

A pungent breath of evergreens.

In a Belfast kitchen
Is Glenn poised
Between cooker and sink
Singing some old pre-war refrain
And cooking something vegetarian?

What
Is Albania's national drink?
Is Fatos braving
The badlands of Tirana for a shot
Of the equivalent of whiskey or gin
With Beshnik?

And Neshe, who
Far away though she is in Cyprus,
I have seen more than once
On Grafton Street turning
Into Brown Thomas to buy a coat
For a cold climate.

Jurica also.
Rucksack on his back
And head in the air,
Peering at houses on Fitzwilliam Square.
Does he pronounce
Them 'good' or 'only colonial'?
Though Jurica too
Is not here.
He is in Croatia.

And that old babushka
Leading her vast but docile cow
On a rope like a pet dog
Glimpsed somewhere on the line between
Saint Petersburg and Moscow –
I hope her painted house
And the cow's byre
Are well-roofed against the snow.

I'd say it must be snowing now.

Now In My Repertoire of Skies

Since then
I have Russia's now
in my repertoire of skies.
Before, I was missing
that alarming skyscape,
high, 'oriental and mysterious'.

That absence of the domestic,
the contented, the nostalgic –
which is to say the melancholic.
Its canopy soars
beyond well-tried 'melancholy'
and its various joys.

Whatever it intends,
rain or shine or old
Muscovy's Asian blue,
this flimsy roof portends pain
and trouble beyond the normal
fears of our insular habitation.

Even the question of the curtains.
Too short to draw
against the northern day-for-night
as, under my blood-red quilt,
I tried to shut my eyes
to the mockery of white.

Now in my repertoire of skies …

Today in Ranelagh Gardens, under
our cloudy vault, homely
as milk, I am assailed
by the malicious ways of the curtain
makers of Saint Petersburg
and an arctic knowledge.

Note to the Ancestors

You'd see, really nothing has changed.

Our weather is just as wilful.
We carry the umbrellas
And still wear the whimsical shoes
You would find much the same.

Gladly like you we fall
Into our beds. Whether sprung
Or of straw, a matter merely
Of one's income or century.

We eat bread, all the stuff
You ate, growing still in fields.
In its dish our soap is veined
From the same dust you inhaled
And we exhale yet
From our mortal cells.

And with your same
Blind or absent gaze we
Stream out of the cinemas,
Wandering along
O'Connell Street like shades.
For we must still content ourselves
With art
Since nobody yet
Has invented the means
To sell us the starring part
In a loved one's dreams.

A Break in the Journey

I like it
Said the traveller girl.
I like the house.

Sure a house is grand.
I like it well.

But she misses the road.

You'd miss the road, she said.
Is there a traveller wouldn't?

So for the few weeks in the summer
she gets in the van and on the road again.

You'd need the break, she said.

A break in the journey.

Acknowledgements

Some of these poems have previously appeared in publications including:

The Irish Times
The Stinging Fly
The Moth
Ranelagh Arts
The SHOp
Storm Force 7
Irish Literature (Poznan)
The Literary Ark (Yerevan)
The Windharp